What Women Can Learn from Men

Sassy Johns

WARNING: If you're a man, you might be insulted by this book

FOR WOMEN ONLY

(AND MEN WITH A SENSE OF HUMOR).

Copyright © 2014 by Sassy Johns
All rights reserved. This book or any portion thereof
may not be reproduced or used in any manner whatsoever
without the express written permission of the publisher,
except for the use of brief quotations in a book review.

*

*

*

*

*

*

*

*

*

*

*

*

*

*

*

*

*

*

*

*

*

*

*

*

*

*

*

*

*

*

*

*

*

*

*

*

*

*

*

*

*

*

*

*

*

*

*

*

*

*

*

*

*

*

*

*

*

*

*

*

*

*

*

*

*

*

*

*

*

*

*

*

*

*

*

*

*

*

*

*

*

*

*

*

*

*

*

*

*

*

*

*

*

*

*

*

If you enjoyed this book, check out its sequel:

50 Reasons Why a Woman Needs a Man

by Sassy Johns

Coming Soon!

Made in the USA
Monee, IL
20 December 2024

74699162R00059